Kid's Bible Day-by-Day

365 Lessons
from the Old
& New Testament

Esther Ra

**Published by Playmore, Inc. Publishers and
Waldman Publishing Corp., New York, New York**

For my Father in heaven, my wonderful family, and for the precious little children of Kahk.

1

FEELING SAD?

• Be joyful whenever you face trials, because testing your faith strengthens you.

James 1:2

• Don't be downcast, my soul. Don't be so disturbed. Put your hope in God, for I will praise my Savior and my God.

Psalm 42:5

• When I was unhappy I called the Lord, and He answered. From deep inside me I called for help, and He heard me.

Jonah 2:2

• Don't be sad. God renews our hearts every day. Our temporary troubles bring us eternal glory that far outweighs our problems. So we fix our eyes not on what is seen, but on what is unseen. Don't be misled by things that are seen, but think that what we see is just for now, and what we don't see is forever.

2 Corinthians 4:16-18

• Be a good soldier for Jesus when you go through hardships.

2 Timothy 2:3

• For a little while it may seem you have all kinds of problems. But this only happens so your faith is proved to be real, and bring you much glory and praise when Jesus is revealed.

1 Peter 1:6-7

• The Lord stays close to the brokenhearted and saves those who are sad in spirit.

Psalm 34:18

2
ANGER AND
FORGIVENESS

• Forgive others if they hurt you.
Forgive them as God forgives you.

Colossians 3:13

• Dear children, we should be quick to listen to others and slow to talk back. Our anger isn't what God wants.

James 1:19-20

• Don't carry your anger overnight. Don't let it make you do what you know inside is wrong.

Ephesians 4:26

- The Lord gets even with His foes and keeps His wrath against His enemies.

Nahum 1:2

- Don't seek to get even or hold a grudge against someone, but love your neighbor as yourself.

Leviticus 19:18

- Don't take revenge, but leave room for God's wrath, for it is written: "It is mine to avenge; I will repay," says the Lord. God will take care of it.

Romans 12:19

• Be good to one another, forgiving each other. Forgive one another, just as through Jesus Christ, God forgives you.

Ephesians 4:32

• Don't let your anger take over. When you are alone and quiet, think about why you are angry and be silent.

Psalm 4:4

• It's smart to use words carefully. Be understanding and even-tempered with others.

Proverbs 17:27

• Help us, God. Because of your Name, forgive our sins.

Psalm 79:9

• God, I make so many mistakes without even knowing it. Please forgive the sins that I may not even know about.

Psalm 19:12

• For the sake of your name, Lord, forgive my wrongs, even though there are so many.   **Psalm 25:11**

- If you forgive others when they hurt you, the heavenly Father will also forgive you. But if you do not forgive others for what they've done wrong to you, then the Father will not forgive your sins.

Matthew 6:14

- If we tell God the things we've done wrong, He will be faithful and just and will forgive us our sins and cleanse us from any bad inside of us.

1 John 1:9

- The wrath of God comes from heaven against all the godlessness and wickedness of men who suppress the truth by their evil doings.

Romans 1:18

FRIENDS

Sometimes a friend can hurt you, but they can still be trusted more than enemies.
Proverbs 27:6

• Good friends make each other better.
Proverbs 27:17

• Two are better than one because if one falls, the other friend can help him up.

Ecclesiastes 4:9-10

• Be encouraging, building each other up.

1 Thessalonians 5:11

• Jesus no longer calls us his servants, but he calls us his friends. He calls us friends because everything he has learned from the Father, he has made known to us.

John 15:15

• Friends love each other through good and bad times.

Proverbs 17:17

SHARING AND CARING

• Those who give, receive. Those who help will be helped.

Proverbs 11:25

• This is love: that God loved us and gave us Jesus His Son, as a sacrifice for everything we've done wrong.

1 John 4:10

• Be the best you can in everything you do, and be as good at giving as you are in everything else you do.

2 Corinthians 8:7

• Give what you want to, not what you have to, because God loves a cheerful giver.

2 Corinthians 9:7

• Jesus himself said, "It is more blessed to give than to receive."

Acts 20:35

If someone asks, give. Do not turn your back on someone who needs to borrow from you.

Matthew 5:42

The more you have been given, the more you will be asked to give.

Luke 12:48

Blessed are those who share their food with poor people.

Proverbs 22:9

Don't put your hope in earthly wealth, because it's so uncertain. Put your hope in God, be rich in good deeds, and be generous and willing to share.

1 Timothy 6:17-19

Give to the poor and needy. Provide for yourselves treasures in heaven. Where your treasure is, so is your heart.

Luke 12:33-34

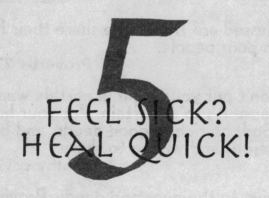

5

FEEL SICK?
HEAL QUICK!

• It's not the healthy who need a doctor but the sick.

Luke 5:31

• God heals us when we hurt.

Psalm 147:3

• Do you feel sick? Friends will pray for you in name of the Lord. Prayer offered in faith helps a sick person get well.

James 5:14-16

• Jesus went throughout Galilee, teaching, preaching, and healing every disease and sickness.

Matthew 4:23

• If we worship God, His blessing will b on us. He will heal sickness, and give you a full life span.

Exodus 23:25-26

• Jesus had compassion for people and healed the sick.

Matthew 14:14

• Elisha sent a messenger to say, "Go, bathe seven times in the River Jordan, and you will be cleansed.

2 Kings 5:10

• Even when all of me fails, God is the strength of my heart and will be forever.

Psalm 73:26

• God will heal us. He will guide us and comfort us, and then we can praise Him.

Isaiah 57:18

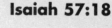

SERVICE FOR THE NERVOUS

• Don't be anxious about things, but by asking in prayer with thanksgiving, present your requests to God. The peace of God, which is above anything you might know, will guide your heart and your mind in Jesus.

Philippians 4:6-7

• Bring Jesus your worries. Cast all of them on Him because He cares for you.

1 Peter 5:7

• God searches me and knows my heart. He tests me and knows all my anxious thoughts.

Psalm 139:23

• When my worries feel great, God comforts me and brings joy to my soul.

Psalm 94:19

7
LET'S FIGHT FRIGHT

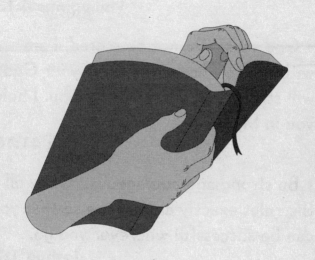

• Remember you can do everything through Him who gives you strength.

Philippians 4:13

• God says, "Do not be scared, I am with you, do not worry, I am your God, I will strengthen you and help you. I hold you in My hands.

Isaiah 41:10

• Be strong and courageous. Obey all the rules exactly as they are so that you can be successful wherever you go.

Joshua 1:7

• God's love has no fear. Perfect love erases fear, because fear is about punishment.

1 John 4:18

• God is my light and my salvation. Whom should I fear? God is the stronghold of my life. Whom should I be afraid of?

Psalm 27:1

• Though I walk through the valley of the shadow of death, I fear no evil, for God is with me. His rod and His staff, they both comfort me.

Psalm 23:4

• Don't be afraid. God redeems you. He calls you by name. You belong to Him.

Isaiah 43:1

• Be confident, remind yourself that the Lord is your helper and don't be afraid.

Hebrews 13:6

A JOYFUL NOISE

- Rejoice in the Lord always.

Philippians 4:4

- Be joyful, pray all the time and give thanks for everything, for this is what God wants.

1 Thessalonians 5:16-18

- Sing to the Lord for His glorious things; tell the world.

Isaiah 12:5

- When your heart is happy, you are cheerful; when your heart aches, it hurts your spirit inside.

Proverbs 15:13

• I delight in God. My soul rejoices in my Lord. He brings me salvation and righteousness.

Isaiah 61:10

• Let's all shout for joy to the Lord. Give Him praise. Come to Him with joyful song.

Psalm 100:1

• A happy heart is like good medicine, but a sad spirit doesn't help you.

Proverbs 17:22

• This is the day the Lord made, let's enjoy it!

Psalm 118:24

• Let's shout for joy to the Lord, so everyone can hear. Let's burst into jubilant song with music; make music to the Lord with harp and sounds of singing.

Psalm 98:4

9

THE BIBLE TALKS TO KIDS

• Whoever welcomes little children in Jesus' name welcomes God. For he who is least will be the greatest.

Luke 9:48

• You must change and become like little children, then you will enter the kingdom of heaven.

Matthew 18:3

• Jesus said, "Let the little children come to me, and do not stop them, for the kingdom of heaven belongs to them."

Matthew 19:14

- Children are their parents' gifts from God and also their reward from Him.
                                                    Psalm 127:3

- God's children are heirs of God and share in God's glory.
                                                    Romans 8:17

- Children, don't let anyone make you do bad things. Do what is right.
                                                    1John 3:7

- Jesus took the children in his arms. He put his hands on them and he blessed them.
                                                    Mark 10:16

• There's no greater joy than to hear that my children are walking in the truth.

3 John 1:4

• Come, my children, listen to me; I will teach you the fear of the Lord. If you love life and want to be good, speak truth, do good, and make peace.

Psalm 34:11-14

• If you believe in Jesus, you can become a child of God.

John 1:12-13

• Teach children well, so that the next generation will know too, so that they can tell their children.

Psalm 78:5-6

10

GOD'S LOVE

• Because the Lord's love is so great, nothing is too much for us. His compassions never fail. Every morning when we wake up, His love is new again, because He is so faithful.

Lamentations 3:22-23

• God shows us His great love because even while we were still sinners, Christ died for us.

Romans 5:8

• God is with you. He takes great delight in loving us with His love. He will rejoice over you with singing.

Zephaniah 3:17

• As God loves us, we should love each other. If we love each other, God's love will be in us.

1 John 4:11-12

• We can always trust in God's unfailing love forever and ever.

Psalm 52:8

• Love is patient, and kind. It doesn't envy. It isn't jealous or bragging. Love isn't proud or rude. It doesn't get angry easily, and it doesn't remember wrongs. Love rejoices with the truth. It'll always protect you, always trust you, always hope in you, and always continue on forever.

1 Corinthians 13:4-7

• God does good things for those who love Him, whom He has called for His purpose.

Romans 8:28

• There's no greater love than Jesus' love, because he laid down His life for us, His friends.

John 15:13

• God's love is deep and wide, long and high, and is greater than any kind of knowledge. Be filled with this love.

Ephesians 3:18-19

• God is good and His love and faithfulness lasts forever, to all the generations.

Psalm 100:5

• When you think you're falling, God's love will support you.

Psalm 94:18

• God will never leave His people. He'll never leave us.

Psalm 94:14

• God is slow to anger and rich in His love for us.

Psalm 145:8

• Stay in God's love as you wait for the mercy of Jesus to bring you to eternal life.

Jude 1:21

• Not even death nor life, nor the present or the future, nor powers, nor height or depth, or anything else in all of creation, can separate us from God's love.

Romans 8:37-38

11
PARENTS-THE FIFTH COMMANDMENT

• Respect your mother and father.

Leviticus 19:3

• Honor your father and your mother, and you'll live long in the land God is giving you.

Exodus 20:12

• Obey your parents. Honor your father and mother is the first commandment with a promise.

Ephesians 6:1-3

• Children, obey your parents, for this is right.

Colossians 3:20

• A wise son learns from his father's teaching.

Proverbs 13:1

• Listen to your father's instruction and don't ever forget what your mother teaches you.

Proverbs 1:8

12

UH OH..

• Everyone's a sinner and all fall short of God's glory.

Romans 3:23

• Don't give up on me, Lord. Please may Your love and truth always protect me.

Psalm 40:11

• O Lord, have mercy on me. Heal me when I have gone against You.

Psalm 41:4

Have mercy on me, O God, with Your never-ending love. With Your compassion wash away all my wrongs, and cleanse me.

Psalm 51:1-2

• On bad days, God keeps me safe in His dwelling.

Psalm 27:5

• Thank You God, that You are our Heavenly Father. You have compassion and comfort. You comfort us in all our troubles. By this we can help those in any trouble with the same comfort You give us.

2 Corinthians 1:3-4

• Teach me, and I will listen; show me how I have been wrong.

Job 6:24

• God is our refuge and strength. No trouble is too much for Him to always help us.

Psalm 46:1-2

• Please God, give me a clean and steady heart and don't cast me from your presence. I want the joy of Your salvation. Give me a willing spirit so I can stand strong.

Psalm 51:10-12

• I know that nothing good lives in my sinful nature. I've the desire to do what is good, but I can't do it.

Romans 7:18

13

RESPECTING OTHERS

• **Don't set yourself above other people, but rather be humble.**

Romans 12:3

• **Show respect to those in charge.**

Romans 13:5

• **Show proper respect to everyone: Love God, the king and the family of believers.**

1 Peter 2:17

Submit to others for Jesus' sake.
Ephesians 5:21

• Show respect for the elderly and show respect for God.
Leviticus 19:32

• If you don't listen, you won't learn and be rewarded.
Proverbs 13:13

• Love the Lord your God with all your heart and with all your soul and all your might. This should be in your hearts.
Deuteronomy 6:5-6

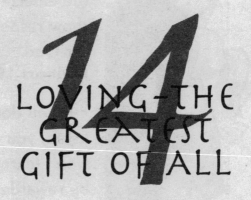

14

LOVING—THE
GREATEST
GIFT OF ALL

- More than anything else, love each other deeply, because love can cover many wrongs.

1 Peter 4:8

- Be sincere when you love others. Don't like things that are evil, but instead do what is good. Be devoted to each other in love and remember to honor others above yourselves.

Romans 12:9-10

- Only one debt can never be paid, the debt to love one another. This is fulfilling God's law.

Romans 13:8

- Love your enemies, do good to those who hate you, bless those who curse you, pray for those who mistreat you.

Luke 6:27-28

• We should love each other as Jesus loves us.

John 15:12

• Treat older people as you would your own parents.

1 Timothy 5:1

• Treat younger men like brothers and younger women like sisters.

1 Timothy 5:1-2

• Live in harmony with one another; be kind and caring.

1 Peter 3:8

Dear children, show your love by your actions, not just with words.

1 John 3:18

15
MAKE EVERY DAY THANKSGIVING

HE LIVES

• I'll praise You forever for what You've done; in Your name I'll hope, for Your name is good. I'll praise You in the presence of Your saints.

Psalm 52:9

• Thank You God, who is the Father of our Lord Jesus Christ. You've blessed us in the heavens with all the spiritual blessings in Jesus.

Ephesians 1:3

I give you praise because I am fearfully and wonderfully made; Your works are wonderful, I know full well.

Psalm 139:14

Praise the Lord! Give thanks to the Lord, for He is so good; His love lasts forever.

Psalm 106:1

O Lord, you are my God; I'll lift up and praise Your name. You're faithful in doing marvelous things, even things planned long, long ago.

Isaiah 25:1

• Give thanks to the Lord, call on His name; tell everyone everywhere about what He has done. Sing praises to Him, as you tell of His wonderful acts.

1 Chronicles 16:8

• Come to God with thanksgiving and with praise in your hearts when you enter God's gates; give thanks to Him and praise His name.

Psalm 100:4

How can I repay the Lord for all His goodness to me? I will lift up the cup of salvation and call on Him.

Psalm 116:12-13

I always thank God for you because of His grace given to you in Christ Jesus.

1 Corinthians 1:4

Let Christ's peace always be in our hearts, since as members of one body you were called to peace. And be thankful.

Colossians 3:15

• Thank you God, for your indescribable gift!

2 Corinthians 9:15

• You're my God, and I'll give You thanks; You're my God, and I'll lift Your name up.

Psalm 118:28

• May the Lord make your love grow more and more so that it overflows for each other and for everyone else around you.

1 Thessalonians 3:12

• Thank You God, for answering me and for becoming My salvation.

Psalm 118:21

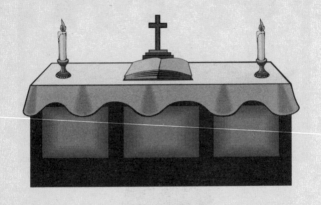

16

HOPE CAN HEAL

• God has plans for us. The Lord tells us His plans to help us and not harm us, to give us hope and a future. When we call upon Him and pray to Him, He listens. When we look for Him with all of our hearts, we will find Him.

Jeremiah 29:11-13

• Be joyful, be patient in suffering, and be faithful in prayer.

Romans 12:12

• Our hope in God is firm, because we know that just as God shares in our hard times, so does He also share in our comfort.

2 Corinthians 1:7

• Blessed is he whose help comes from the God of Jacob. If your hope is in the Lord his God, the Maker of everything you see, He remains faithful to us forever.

Psalm 146:5

• Praise be to God, Father of our Lord Jesus Christ! With His great mercy, He has given us new life into a living hope through the resurrection of Jesus Christ from the dead. This will be kept in heaven for us forever.

1 Peter 1:3-4

• When you go through hard times, according to God's will, you should still stay committed to our faithful Creator and continue to do good.

1 Peter 4:19

• And hope does not disappoint us, because God filled our hearts with love by the Holy Spirit, whom He has provided for us.

Romans 5:5

• If you hope for what you don't have, then wait for it patiently.

Romans 8:25

17
WHY WORRYING DOESN'T WORK

• Take delight in the Lord and He'll give you what your heart desires.

Psalm 37:4

• Wait for God; be strong and take heart as you wait for Him.

Psalm 27:14

• Trust in the Lord forever, for He is the Rock that will never disappear.

Isaiah 26:4

Do not love money, but be happy with what you have, because God has said, "Never will I leave you; never will I forsake you.

Hebrews 13:5

Sovereign Lord, You have made the heavens and the earth with Your great power and outstretched arm. Nothing is too hard for You.

Jeremiah 32:17

• In Jesus, you can have peace. Here on earth, you'll have trouble. But take heart! Jesus has overcome the world.

John 16:33

• Nothing is impossible with God.

Luke 1:37

• Don't worry about your life, about what you will eat or drink or what you will wear. Isn't life more important than clothes? God even takes care of the birds in the air and you're much more important than they are. Worrying doesn't help you, so don't worry.

Matthew 6:25-27

18
BROTHERS AND SISTERS

• If you don't take care of your family, especially your parents and brothers and sisters, you have turned away from the faith. This is worse than being a non-believer.

1 Timothy 5:8

• When someone does something wrong to you, don't do something wrong back to them. Instead, always try to be kind to each other and to everyone else.

1 Thessalonians 5:15

• When someone does something mean to you, don't repay them with evil or insults, but instead by doing something kind.

1 Peter 3:9

• Do nothing to raise yourself higher, but in humility consider others better than yourself. You should look not only to what you want, but also to what others want.

Philippians 2:3-4

• The Lord will bless you and keep you safe; the Lord will look to you with favor, be gracious to you; and give you peace.

Numbers 6:24-26

• Since there's jealousy and fighting among you, you're still worldly. You're acting like mere men.

1 Corinthians 3:3

19

SCHOOL LIFE

• Even though you're young, don't let anyone look down on you, but be a good role model for others as you speak, as you live, as you love, as you believe, and as you are pure.
1 Timothy 4:12

• Make it your goal to lead a quiet life, to mind your own busines and to work with your hands. Then your daily life will win the respect of outsiders, and you won't depend on anybody.
1 Thessalonians 4:11

• We pray that you may live a life worthy of the Lord and please Him in every way: showing fruit in every good work and learning more about God.

Colossians 1:10

• Commit to the Lord everything you do, then your plans will be successful.

Proverbs 16: 3

• Whether you eat or drink or whatever you do, give God the glory.

1 Corinthians 10:31

• Do things that are good for everybody, as you try to please everybody in every way. Don't just look after your own good but look after the good of many, so that they can be saved. Follow the example of Christ.

1 Corinthians 10:32-11:1

• Live as children of the light who show goodness, righteousness and truth.

Find out what pleases God and do it.

Ephesians 5:8-9

• Try your best to live in peace with everybody and be holy; without holiness you will never see the Lord.

Hebrews 12:14

• With whatever you do, when you talk or do other activities with others, do it in Jesus' name. Don't forget to thank God for Jesus too.

Colossians 3:17

• May everything I say and everything I think be pleasing to You, God. You are my rock and my redeemer.

Psalm 19:14

• God has shown me what is good. God doesn't want us to do anything but to act justly and to love mercy and to walk humbly with Him.

Micah 6:8

20
THE LESSON OF
PATIENCE

• A patient person shows great under-standing, but a quick-tempered one doesn't.

Proverbs 14:29

• Be completely humble and gentle; be patient, bearing with one another in love. Make every effort to keep the unity of the Spirit through the bond of peace.

Ephesians 4:2-3

• The end of a matter is better than its beginning, and patience is better than pride.

Ecclesiastes 7:8

• A hot-tempered man causes trouble, but a patient man calms things down.

Proverbs 15:18

• Patience is better than being the best fighter; a person who controls his temper is better than one who conquers land.

Proverbs 16:32

• The more you know, the more patient you'll be.

Proverbs 19:11

• Be strengthened with God's power so that you may have great endurance and patience, and joyfully give thanks to our God, the Father, who wants you to share in the blessings in the kingdom of light.

Colossians 1:12

• Warn people who are lazy, encourage those who are shy, help the ones who are weak, and be patient with everyone.

1 Thessalonians 5:14

God stands far from bad people, but
he hears the prayer of the good people.

Proverbs 15:29

Sit still before God and wait patiently
for him; don't worry when others seem
as if they're doing better than you are,
especially if they do it in dishonest
ways.

Psalm 37:7

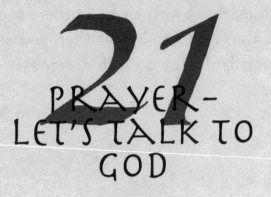

21

PRAYER –
LET'S TALK TO
GOD

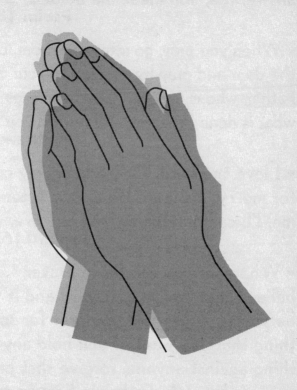

• When I pray, You hear me and You answer me; You made me bolder.

Psalm 138:3

• When you pray, go into your room, close the door and pray by yourself to your Father, who is unseen. God, who sees what is done in secret, will reward you.

Matthew 6:6

• I love the Lord, for He hears my cries for mercy. Because He always listens to me, I'll call on Him as long as I live.

Psalm 116:1-2

• Whatever you ask for in prayer, believe that you've gotten it, and it will be yours. And when you pray for something that you want, if you hold anything against anyone, forgive that person, so that your Father in heaven may forgive you and your sins.

Mark 11: 24-25

• And pray in the spirit at all different times, asking all kinds of prayer and requests. With this in mind, keep praying for everyone. Pray also that whenever you open your mouth, you can share the gospel boldly as an ambassador. Pray that you may declare it fearlessly.

Ephesians 6:18-19

Requests, prayers, intercession and thanksgiving should be made for everyone, including kings and all those in authority, that we may live peacefully and quietly, lives full in all godliness and holiness.

1 Timothy 2:1

• Pray always!

1 Thessalonians 5:17

 • And when you pray, don't show off to men, but pray with a sincere heart for God.

Matthew 6:5

• This is how God teaches us to pray: "Our Father in heaven, hallowed be Your name, Your kingdom come, Your will be done, on earth, as it is in heaven. Give us today our daily bread. Forgive us of our sin, as we forgive those who sin against us. And lead us not into temptation, but deliver us from the evil one."

Matthew 6:9-13

• Be devoted to prayer, be watchful, and say thank you.

Colossians 4:2

• Pray that we may be protected from evil. Not everyone has faith, but the Lord is always faithful and He will strengthen and protect you from the evil one.

2 Thessalonians 3:2

• Tell each other what you've done wrong and pray for each other so that you may be healed. The prayer of the righteous is powerful and effective.

James 5:16

• Please answer me when I call to You, O God. Give me relief from my troubles; be merciful to me and hear my prayer.

Psalm 4:1

• The Lord promises if we call to Him, He will answer us, telling us about great and unsearchable things we don't know.

Jeremiah 33:3

22

WHEN IN DOUBT

• A simple person believes anything, but a prudent man thinks about the steps he'll take.

Proverbs 14:15

• When you pray, you must believe and not doubt, because if you doubt, it is like the waves of the sea being blown and tossed around by the wind. You should not expect to receive anything from the Lord if you're thinking two different things and are unstable in what you do.

James 1:6-8

• Jesus said that if you have faith and do not doubt, anything can be done. You could even say to a mountain, "Go, throw yourself in the sea," and it could be done. If you truly believe, you will get whatever you ask for in prayer.

Matthew 21:21-22

• Jesus said that people who saw him, believed in him; blessed are those who have not seen Jesus and yet have believed.

John 20:29

• Have mercy toward those who doubt.

Jude 1:22

• Make sure that none of you has a sinful, unbelieving heart that turns away from the living God.

Hebrews 3:12

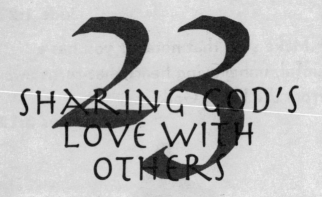

23
SHARING GOD'S LOVE WITH OTHERS

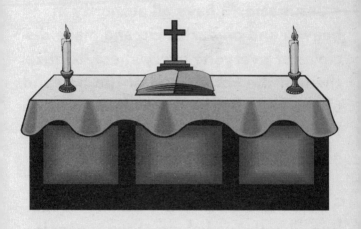

• Share and take care of God's people who are in need. Show them hospitality.
Romans 12:13

• Jesus said, "I have all authority in heaven and on earth. Go and make disciples of everyone everywhere, baptize them in the Father, and of the Son and of the Holy Spirit. Teach them to listen to everything I've told you. Surely I'm always with you, to the very end."
Matthew 28:18-20

• Jesus said if we come and follow him, he will make us fishers of men, people who help others know about God's love.
Matthew 4:19

• You're a light in this world. Just like a city on a hill cannot be hidden, you can't light a lamp and then put it under a bowl. Instead, put it on a stand, so that everyone can see. In the same way, let your light shine before other people, so that they can see the good things that you do and praise God in heaven.

Matthew 5:14-16

• We receive power when the Holy Spirit comes. We'll be God's witnesses to every single place all over the earth.

Acts 1:8

• The message of Jesus' love for us will be shared to everyone in the whole world. Then the end will come.

Matthew 24:14

Share everything you have seen and heard with everyone you know, not just your friends.

Acts 22:1

• God loved the world so much that He gave us His one and only Son, that whoever believes in Him will not die but will live forever in heaven.

John 3:16

• Every knee should bow at Jesus' name, in heaven and on earth and under the earth, and every tongue should say that Jesus Christ is Lord, so that it glorifies God the Father.

Philippians 2:9-11

• You are like salt that brings flavor to this world.

Matthew 5:13

• My life is worth nothing to me, unless I can finish the race and complete the task Jesus has given me of sharing the gospel of God's grace to others.

Acts 20:24

• I'm not ashamed of the gospel, because it's the power of God for the salvation of everyone who believes.

Romans 1:16

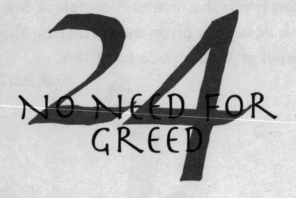

24
NO NEED FOR GREED

• Jesus said, "Be careful! Watch out for all kinds of greed, because life is not about how many things you have."

Luke 12:15

• You can be sure that no greedy person has any part in the kingdom of Christ and of God.

Ephesians 5:5

• People who want to get rich begin to do bad things and give into many foolish and harmful desires that could ruin them. The love of money is the bottom of all kinds of bad things. People who only want money wander and get into trouble.

1 Timothy 6:9-10

$ $ $

• Take care of God's people like a shepherd watches his sheep, not because you have to, but because you want to be as God would want you to be. Don't be greedy for money, but be willing to serve as good examples to others.

1 Peter 5:2

• If you always do things honestly, you'll be safe, but if you don't, someone will find out about the dishonest things you do.

Proverbs 10:9

25
REST ASSURED

When I go to sleep, I will not worry, because you, O Lord, always keep me safe from all harm.

Psalm 4:8

• Jesus tells us to go to him when we are tired and need a break and he will give us the rest we need. Learn from Him, because he is gentle and humble in heart, and then you will find rest for your soul.

Matthew 11:28-29

• Since God promises us that we can enter into rest, be careful that we don't take it for granted.

Hebrews 4:1

• My soul finds rest in you alone, God; my salvation comes from you too.

Psalm 62:1

• God tells us that He will always be with us no matter where we go and that He will give us rest.

Exodus 33:14

• My soul finds rest in God alone and my hope comes from Him. He alone is my rock and my salvation; He is the surest thing I know, so I'll never fall down.

Psalm 62:5-6

• Six days out of the seven days, we should work, but on the seventh day, we should rest because it is a Sabbath of rest. God is holy.

Exodus 31:15

If you stay in God's shelter, He'll give ou rest in His shadows.

Psalm 91:1

There's a Sabbath day of rest for God's people; for anyone who enters God's rest also rests from his own work, ust as God did from His.

Hebrews 4:9-10

When you get tired, think of Jesus nd all that He went through, then you von't grow weary and be discouraged.

Hebrews 12:3

26

THE BIBLE TELLS US SC

• God helped men write all Scripture so that we can use it for teaching, correcting and training in righteousness, so that we can be ready for any good work at any time.

2 Timothy 3:16

• How can you keep your way pure? By living according to God's words in the Bible.

Psalm 119:9

• Above anything else, know that the words of the Bible did not come from the writer's own view, but God spoke to writers through the Holy Spirit so that they could write.

2 Peter 1:20-21

• We can't live life only with bread to eat, but we also need every word that comes from God.

Matthew 4:4

• Your word is like a lamp to guide my feet and a light to guide my path.

Psalm 119:105

• Until Jesus comes again, make sure you read, teach, and preach God's word out loud to others.

1 Timothy 4:13

• Take delight in God's words. Think about them all day as you go to school or and play, and all night as you sleep.

Psalm 1:2

• I hide Your word, God, inside my heart so that with its help, I won't do bad things against You.

Psalm 119:11

• God's word is living and active. It's sharper than the sharpest sword, and it can even penetrate your most secret thoughts and divide soul and spirit, joints and marrow. It judges the thought and attitudes inside your heart.

Hebrews 4:12

• Each and every word of God is perfect without any mistakes; He protects those who go to Him.

Proverbs 30:5

• Let Christ's word stay with you as you teach and correct each other with wisdom. Sing psalms, hymns, and spiritual songs thanking God.

Colossians 3:16

• Keep these words of God forever in your hearts.

Deuteronomy 11:18

Your word, O Lord, is forever; it stands secure in the heavens.

Psalm 119:89

Simon Peter asked Jesus, "Who should I go to? You have the words about having eternal life."

John 6:68

Even if heaven and earth disappear, Jesus' words will never disappear.

Matthew 24:35

Be like the wise builder who go and hears Jesus' words and then puts them to good practice.

Luke 6:47

Your words are so sweet, Lord, sweeter than honey in my mouth.

Psalm 119:103

27
HEAVEN HAS A PLACE FOR YOU

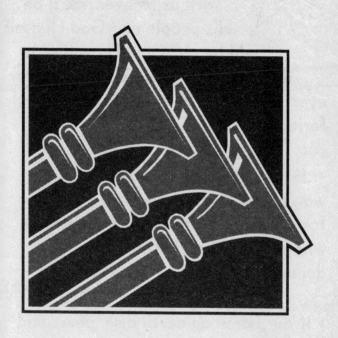

• In heaven, God will live with us forever. We'll be His people and God Himself will be our God. He will wipe every tear that falls down from our eyes. There will be no more hurt or suffering.

Revelation 21:3-4

• Jesus said, "The kingdom of God won't come even if we wait and watch for it carefully, and people can't say where it is either, because God's kingdom can be found within you.

Luke 17:20-21

• If our home on earth disappears and gets ruined, remember that we have a home with God forever in the heavens, not built by humans.

2 Corinthians 5:1

Will God stay on earth? How can He when even the widest heavens can't hold Him?

1 Kings 8:27

• God says He will create a new place with new heavens and earth. Things from before won't be remembered. There will never again be a child who lives but a few days, or a man who does not live to be old. In heaven, he who dies at the age of a hundred will be thought of as a young person. They'll not work for nothing or have children who will face trouble in their lives. In heaven, we'll be blessed by the Lord, and so will our children and their children.

Isaiah 65:17-23

• Those who pursue God's desire for righteousness will inherit the kingdom of heaven.

Matthew 5:10

• Don't collect treasures here on earth that can disappear; instead store up for yourselves treasures in heaven, where even moths and rust can't destroy it and where thieves don't break in and steal it.

Matthew 6:19-20

• When Jesus comes, the angels will come with him and he'll sit on his throne in heavenly glory while all the nations sit before him.

Matthew 25:31-32

• Always remember to do one thing: Forget the past and strain toward what is ahead. Press on toward the goal, to win the prize which God has given to us in heaven through Christ Jesus.

Philippians 3:14

• Jesus said, "No one who looks back is fit for service in the kingdom of God."

Luke 9:62

28
FINDING PEACE

• Jesus tells us, "Peace I leave with you, peace I give you. I don't give to you as the world gives, so don't let your heart be troubled and don't be afraid."

John 14:27

• Try to be good and listen to God. Then the God of love and peace will be with you.

2 Corinthians 13:11

• Those who sow in peace raise a harvest of righteousness.

James 3:18

• The Lord gives strength to His people by blessing His people with His peace.

Psalm 29:11

Make sure whatever you have learned or heard from Jesus, or seen, that you put it into practice daily. And the God of peace will be with you.

Philippians 4:9

Keep in perfect peace God's steadfast mind, because He trusts in you.

Isaiah 26:3

Those who are peacemakers are blessed, for God calls them His children.

Matthew 5:9

God is not a God of disorder but a God of peace.

1 Corinthians 14:33

29

WHAT THE HOLY SPIRIT TEACHES US

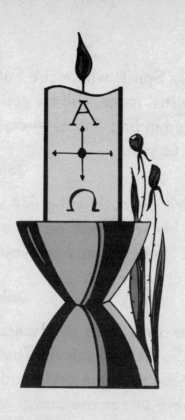

• The Holy Spirit, whom the Father will send in Jesus' name, will be your teacher, reminding you of everything I have said to you.

John 14:26

• The Spirit of truth will guide you into all truth. He will speak on his own and only what he hears, and tell you about what hasn't come yet.

John 16:13

• God anointed Jesus of Nazareth with the Holy Spirit and power. That's how he went around doing good and healing all who were under the power of the devil, because God was with him.

Acts 10:38

The Lord is the Spirit, and where the Spirit is, there is freedom.

2 Corinthians 3:17

• No eye has seen, no ear has heard, and no mind knows what God has prepared for those who love him.

1 Corinthians 2:9

• God has revealed His Spirit to us. The Spirit searches everything, even the deep things of God.

1 Corinthians 2:10

• No one knows the thoughts of man except the Spirit of God.

1 Corinthians 2:11

In the Holy Spirit, there are fruits: love, joy, peace, patience, kindness, goodness, faithfulness, gentleness, and self-control. There are no laws against such things.

Galatians 5:22

• Dear friends, pray in the Holy Spirit so that you can become more holy in faith.

Jude 1:20

• In the same way, the Holy Spirit helps us when we are weak. When we don't know what to pray for, the Spirit himself helps us to pray.

Romans 8:26

• God created you. Your body is a temple of the Holy Spirit, who is in you, whom God gave you. You don't own yourselves, so respect your body and be respectful to God with your body.

1 Corinthians 6:19

• God will always keep us. We know that because He put His Spirit in our hearts to promise what is to come.

2 Corinthians 1:22

30
LEARN TO LIVE, LIVE TO LEARN

• Wisdom is supreme; therefore get wisdom. Even if it costs all you have, get understanding.

Proverbs 4:7

• The Lord gives wisdom, and from Him comes knowledge and understanding.

Proverbs 2:6

• The fear of God is the beginning of knowledge. Only fools despise wisdom and discipline.

Proverbs 1: 7

• Pay attention and learn. Listen to words of knowledge.

Proverbs 23:12

• A person who is wise shows it by his good life, by good deeds done in humility that comes from wisdom.

James 3:13

• Wisdom that comes from heaven is pure; then it is peace-loving, considerate, submissive, full of mercy and good fruit, not showing favoritism and genuine in knowledge.

James 3:11

• Hold on to the lesson you learn; don't let it go, guard it well, for it is your life.

Proverbs 4:13

• Instruct a wise man and he becomes wiser; teach a righteous man and he will learn even more.

Proverbs 9:9

31
GOING TO CHURCH

• Let's not stop meeting together, as some do, but let's encourage one another—and all the more as you see the Day approaching.

Hebrews 10:25

• So when Peter was kept in prison, the church prayed to God to help him.

Acts 12:5

• Christ loved the church and gave himself up for everyone in it.

Ephesians 5:25

• If you are eager to have spiritual gifts, try to excel in gifts that build up the church.

1 Corinthians 14:12

• Watch over God's church, just as God watches over it as His own.

Acts 20:28

• Don't forget that Jesus is in charge of all the people who believe and also in charge of the church.

Colossians 1:18

• One thing I ask, Lord, this is what I seek: that I may stay in the Lord's house every single day of my life, to gaze at the beauty of the Lord and to seek Him in His church.

Psalm 27:4

• Don't you know that you're God's temple and that God's Spirit lives in you? If anyone destroys God's temple, God will destroy him because His temple is precious and sacred, and you're that temple.

1 Corinthians 3:16-17

32
KEEP ON KEEPING ON!

- God will help direct you with His love and Christ's perseverance.

2 Thessalonians 3:5

- Blessed are those who persevere under trial. When you stand the test, you will receive the crown of life promised to us who love Him.

James 1:12

- Don't become tired of doing good! When it's time, we'll reap a harvest if we don't give up. As we can, let's do good to all people.

Galatians 6:9

- Stand firm and don't let anything move you. Always give yourselves fully to the Lord's work because you know what you do for God isn't without a purpose.

1 Corinthians 15:58

- We also rejoice when we go through

hard times, because we know the hard times produces perseverance; perseverance produces character; and character produces hope.

Romans 5:3-4

• Let's come close to God willingly with complete faith, free from any guiltiness. Let's hold on without forgetting our hope in Jesus. Remember he promised to be faithful.

Hebrews 10:22-23

• Keep on trying so that when you have done God's will, you will receive what He promised.

Hebrews 10:36

• Let's give up everything that keeps us back and the evil that's inside of our hearts, and let us keep running the race marked out for us.

Hebrews 12:1

33
FAITH CAN WORK WONDERS

- Faith is what we hope for, believing in things we haven't seen.

Hebrews 11:1

- We live by believing in God and not by what we see.

2 Corinthians 5:7

- Since I heard about your faith in Jesus and your love for all who believe in Him, I've not stopped thanking God for you and remembering you in my prayers.

Ephesians 1:15

- Just as your body without the spirit is dead, faith without deeds is also dead.

James 2:26

Jesus said even when we have little faith, if we have faith as small as a mustard seed, it can move mountains! Nothing will be impossible.

Matthew 17:20

We're saved by grace through faith. This doesn't come from yourself, but is the gift of God. So, no matter what you do, you can't be saved by doing good, but only by God's grace.

Ephesians 2:8-9

Have faith in God and then you will be successful.

2 Chronicles 20:20

• We have faith as we hear the message, and we hear the message through the word of Christ.

Romans 10:1

• Without faith we can't please God, because if we come to Him we believe He exists and He rewards us for earnestly seeking him.

Hebrews 11:6

• Don't judge others who have weaker faiths; instead, accept them.

Romans 14:3

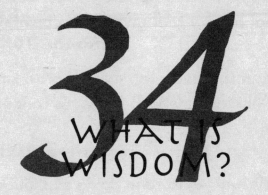

34

WHAT IS WISDOM?

- The wise in heart accept commands, but the one who talks too much comes to ruin.

Proverbs 10:8

- Wise men store up knowledge, but the mouth of a fool invites his downfall.

Proverbs 10:14

- When there are too many words, sin is not absent. He who holds his tongue is wise.

Proverbs 10:19

- Fools find pleasure in doing evil, but a man of understanding delights in wisdom.

Proverbs 10:23

• Counsel and sound judgment are God's characteristics. He has understanding and power.

Proverbs 8:14

• Wisdom is supreme, so try to get wisdom. Though it costs you everything you have, get understanding.

Proverbs 4:7

• You desire truth inside. You teach me wisdom in the inmost place.

Psalm 51:6

• The Spirit of the Lord will rest on you. This includes the Spirit of wisdom and of understanding, the Spirit of counsel and of power, the Spirit of knowledge and of the fear of the Lord.

Isaiah 11:2

• If you lack wisdom, ask God, who gives generously to all without finding fault, and He will give it.

James 1:5

• Blessed is the man who finds wisdom, for he gains understanding.

Proverbs 3:13

Pride only stirs fights, but wisdom is found in those who take advice.

Proverbs 13:10

A man who loves wisdom makes his father happy.

Proverbs 29:3

Wisdom is more precious than even the most expensive rubies.

Proverbs 8:11

35

HONEST TO GOODNESS

- If you can be trusted with very little, you can also be trusted with very much, but if you are dishonest with very little you'll also be dishonest with very much.

Luke 16:10

- The integrity of those who are good guides them, but the unfaithful are destroyed by their double lives.

Proverbs 11:3

- I know, God, that You test the heart and are pleased with integrity. I have given You all these things willingly and with honest intent. And now I have seen with joy how willingly Your people have given to You.

1 Chronicles 29:17

- Don't be dishonest when measuring length, weight, or quantity.

Leviticus 19:35

- Dishonest money goes away, but if you gather money little by little, it'll grow.

Proverbs 13:11

- The righteous don't like the dishonest and the wicked don't like the upright.

Proverbs 29:27

36

BUILDING TRUST

- Into our hands, I give You my Spirit; make me better, Lord, the God of truth.

Psalm 31:5

- If you trust in Him, you'll never be put to shame.

1 Peter 2:6

- I hate those who hold on to worthless idols; I trust in the Lord.

Psalm 31: 6

- We who know Your name will trust in You, for You, Lord, never forsake those who seek You.

Psalm 9:10

- Stop trusting in man, who merely breathes through his nostrils. Who is he to tell you what to do?

Isaiah 2:22

- Jesus trusts in God. God will rescue Him if he wants to, for he said, I am the Son of God.

Matthew 27:43

- O Lord Almighty, the one who trusts in You is blessed.

Psalm 84:12

- The one who trusts in the Lord, whose confidence is in Him is blessed.

Jeremiah 17:7

37

PROMISES

- None of the Lord's good promises to the house of Israel failed.

Joshua 21:45

- You know with all your heart and soul that not a single one of all the good promises the Lord your God gave you ever failed. Every promise has been fulfilled; not a single one has failed.

Joshua 23:14

- I will listen to what God will say; He promises peace to His people, His saints, but only if they don't return to evil.

Psalm 85:8

- God's not a man, that He should lie, nor a son of man, that He would change His mind. Does He speak and then not act? Does He ever promise and not fulfill?

Numbers 23:19

- My comfort in hard trials is this: Your promise preserves my life.

Psalm 119:50

- Your kingdom is a kind of kingdom that lasts forever, and your dominion endures through all generations. He's faithful to all His promises and loving toward all He has made.

Psalm 145:13

- The Lord's not slow in keeping his promise, as some are. He's patient, not wanting anyone to die without knowing Him, but desires everyone to come to repentance.

2 Peter 3:9

- With God's promise, we look forward to a new heaven and a new earth, the home of righteousness.

2 Peter 3:13

- The Lord will bless you as He promised, and you'll help many nations, but will borrow from none.

Deuteronomy 15:6

- No matter how many promises God makes, they are always "Yes" in Christ. And we say "Amen" to give glory to God.

2 Corinthians 1:20

• Faith and knowledge rest on the hope of eternal life, which God, who doesn't lie, promised before the beginning of time.

Titus 1:2

• Since we have these promises, let's purify ourselves from everything that makes our body and spirit dirty, perfecting holiness out of respect for God.

2 Corinthians 7:1

38
LIFE ETERNAL

• If you hear the words of Jesus, and believe Him who sent Jesus has eternal life, you will not be condemned; you have crossed over from death to eternal life.

John 5:24

• No one can enter the kingdom of God unless he is born of water and the Holy Spirit.

John 3:3

• Don't forget one thing: When we're with the Lord, a day will be like a thousand years, and a thousand years will be like a day.

2 Peter 3:8

- God appointed me from eternity, from the very beginning, even before the world began.

Proverbs 8:23

- Eternal life is that you may know the only true God and Jesus Christ, whom God sent.

John 17:3

- God gives us eternal life, and this life is in His Son. He who has the Son, has life.

1 John 5:11

- God remains the same, and His years will never end. The children of His servants will live in His presence; their descendants will be established before Him.

Psalm 102:27-28

• My Father's will is that everyone who looks to the Son and believes in Him will have eternal life, and He'll raise him up on the last day.

John 6:40

• On the last day, we who are still alive and are left will be caught up together in the clouds to meet the Lord in the air. We'll be with the Lord forever. Encourage each other with these words.

1 Thessalonians 4:17-18

• He has made everything beautiful in His time. He has also set eternity in the hearts of men; yet they can't under-stand what God has done from begin-ning to end.

Ecclesiastes 3:11

HAPPINESS IS...

39

• I'm not saying this because I'm in need, for I've learned to be content in whatever circumstances. I know what it is to be in need, and I know what it is to have plenty. I've learned the secret of being content in any and every situation, whether well fed or hungry, whether rich or poor.

Philippians 4:11-12

• Whoever loves money will never have enough; whoever loves wealth will never be satisfied with his income. This also doesn't have any meaning.

Ecclesiastes 5:10

- Godliness with contentment is great gain. We brought nothing into the world, and we can't take anything out of it. But if we have food and clothing, we'll be content with that. People who want to get rich fall into temptation and into many foolish and harmful desires that ruin them.

1 Timothy 6:8-9

Behold... The Lord

• As goods and treasures increase, so do those who consume them. And what good are they to you, except to feast your eyes on them?

Ecclesiastes 5:11

• I know there's nothing better for us than to be happy and do good while we live. Everyone can eat and drink, and find satisfaction in work—this is the gift of God.

Ecclesiastes 3:12-13

Look for
all the
titles in this
series

KID'S BIBLE DAY-BY-DAY
$1.95
$2.75 Can./Aust.

365 FACTS

FROM THE OLD AND NEW TESTAMENTS

KID'S BIBLE DAY-BY-DAY
$1.95
$2.75 Can./Aust.

365 LESSONS

FROM THE OLD AND NEW TESTAMENTS

KID'S BIBLE DAY-BY-DAY
$1.95
$2.75 Can./Aust.

365 PEOPLE

FROM THE OLD AND NEW TESTAMENTS

KID'S BIBLE DAY-BY-DAY
$1.95
$2.75 Can./Aust.

365 PROMISES

FROM THE OLD AND NEW TESTAMENTS

SR-SR / 5520-2 / 2750 / 192